WAR & GENOCIDE

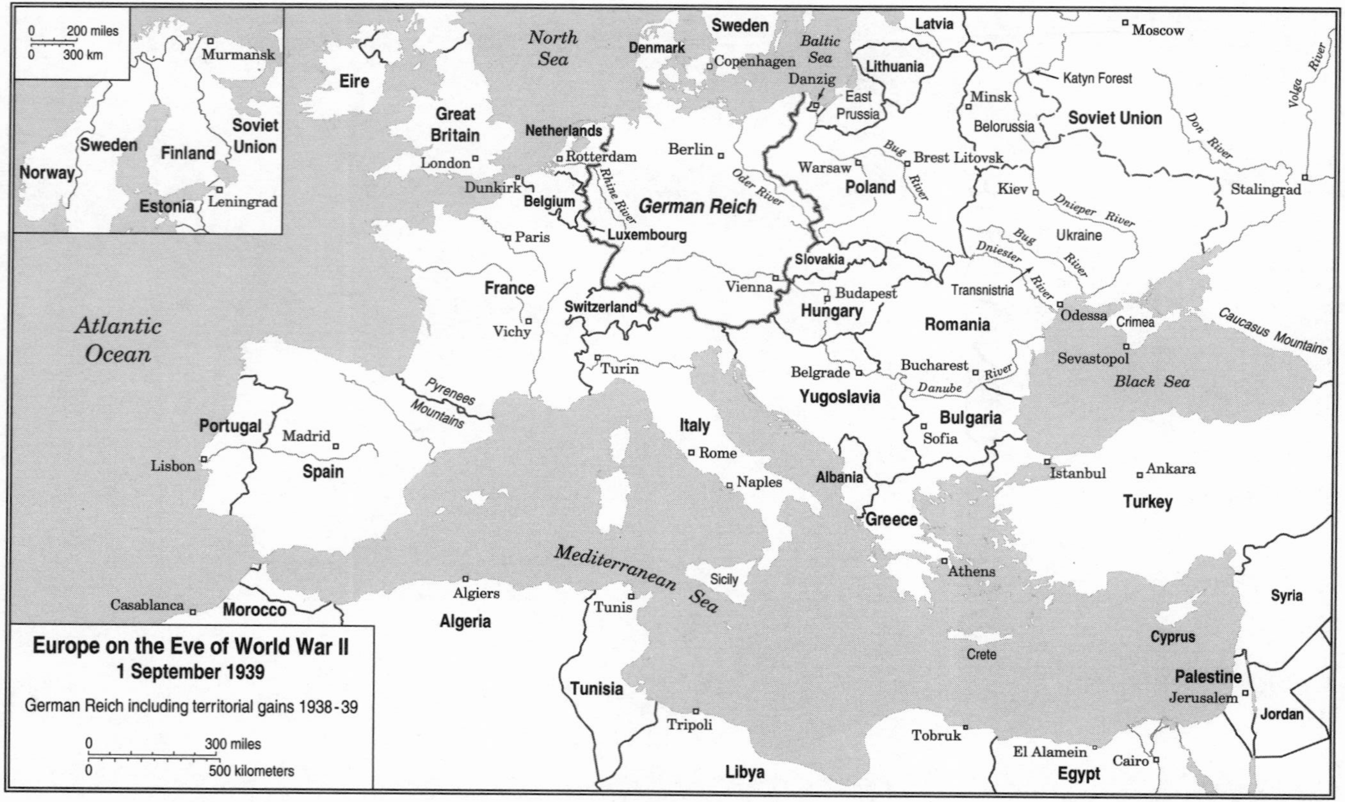

Europe on the Eve of World War II
1 September 1939

German Reich including territorial gains 1938-39

Map by Michael J. Fisher, cartographer